This book is dedicated to my family.
Especially to my grandfather, my grandmother, and my mother,
because I would have never become anything if not thanks to them.

And also to you, the reader, because without you
I would have never found the happiness that I was looking for ✨

–   Sincerely, Alex Casillas

Introduction

Welcome to the comprehensive guide to learning JavaScript! This book is designed to help you acquire the essential skills and knowledge you need to jumpstart your career as a JavaScript developer. Whether you are a complete beginner or have some experience with coding, this book will take you on a journey through the basics of JavaScript and its key features.

JavaScript is one of the most popular and widely-used programming languages in the world, and it plays a critical role in the development of dynamic web pages and applications. With its versatility and ease of use, JavaScript has become a must-know skill for developers who want to build web-based solutions that are engaging, interactive, and responsive.

In this book, you will learn everything you need to know about JavaScript, including its syntax, data types, operators, control structures, functions, arrays, objects, and more. This book will provide you with hands-on experience, from simple scripts to complex applications.

By the end of this book, you will have a solid foundation in JavaScript programming, and you will be ready to tackle more advanced topics and projects. Whether you are interested in freelancing, working for a company, or pursuing a career in web development, this book will provide you with the skills and confidence you need to succeed. So, get ready to learn, code, and launch your JavaScript career!

Variables in JavaScript

A variable is a named storage location in a computer program where values can be stored and retrieved. Variables are used to store data, such as numbers, strings, or arrays, and manipulate that data in a program. In JavaScript, a variable is declared using the `var`, `let`, or `const` keyword, followed by a unique identifier that serves as the name of the variable.

```
const message = "Hello, World!";
```

In the example above, `message` is the name of the variable, and `"Hello, World!"` is the value that is stored in the variable. Variables can be used and reassigned throughout the code, allowing values to be stored, manipulated, and retrieved as needed.

Undefined

The `undefined` type in JavaScript is a value that represents the absence of a value or a variable that has been declared but has not been assigned a value.

When a variable is declared but has no value assigned to it, its value is `undefined`. For instance:

```
const x;
console.log(x); // Logs "undefined"
```

In the example above, the variable `x` is declared but has no value assigned to it, so its value is `undefined`.

It's also possible to explicitly set a variable to `undefined` by assigning the value `undefined` to it:

```
const y = undefined;
console.log(y); // Logs "undefined"
```

In JavaScript, the value `undefined` is not the same as the value `null`. `null` represents an intentional non-value, while `undefined` represents a lack of value.

Boolean

A `Boolean` in JavaScript is a data type that has only two possible values: `true` and `false`. It is often used in conditional statements and loops to control the flow of a program based on whether a certain condition is true or false. For instance:

```
const x = true;
const y = false;
```

In the example above, `x` is assigned the value `true` and `y` is assigned the value `false`.

Booleans are often used in conditional statements to test conditions and execute code based on the result of the test. For instance:

```
const isTrue = true;

if (isTrue) {
  console.log("The condition is true");
}
```

In the example above, the condition `isTrue` is evaluated to be `true`, so the code inside the `if` statement will be executed, and `"The condition is true"` will be logged to the console.

It's also possible to compare values using comparison operators (such as `<`, `>`, `==`, `===`, etc.), and the result of the comparison will be a `Boolean` value. For instance:

```
const a = 10;
const b = 20;
const result = a < b;
console.log(result); // logs "true"
```

In the example above, the expression `a < b` evaluates to `true` since `10` is less than `20`. The result of the comparison is stored in the variable result, which has a value of `true`.

Number

The `Number` type in JavaScript is a numeric data type that can represent both integers and floating-point numbers. In JavaScript, all numbers are represented as floating-point numbers, even if they are integers. For instance:

```
const x = 42;
const y = 3.14;
console.log(x); // Logs "42"
console.log(y); // Logs "3.14"
```

In the example above, `x` is assigned the integer value `42`, and `y` is assigned the floating-point value `3.14`.

JavaScript provides several methods for working with numbers, such as mathematical operations (e.g., addition, subtraction, multiplication, etc.), conversion between different number formats (e.g., a string to a number), and rounding of decimal values. For instance:

```
const a = 10;
const b = 20;
const result = a + b;
console.log(result); // Logs "30"
```

In the example above, the expression `a + b` adds the values of `a` and `b` (`10 + 20`), and the result of the expression is stored in the variable `result`, which has a value of `30`.

It's also important to note that JavaScript has special numeric values, such as `Infinity` and `-Infinity`, which represent positive and negative infinity, and `NaN` (Not-a-Number), which represents the result of a mathematical operation that is undefined or unrepresentable.

BigInt

`BigInt` is a new primitive type in JavaScript that was introduced in ECMAScript 2020 (ES11). It allows you to represent arbitrarily large integers, as opposed to the `Number` type, which has limited precision and can only accurately represent integers up to ($2^{53} - 1$). For instance:

```
const x = 9007199254740991n;
console.log(x); // Logs "9007199254740991n"
```

In the example above, the `BigInt` value `9007199254740991n` is assigned to the constant `x`. Note that the `n` suffix is used to indicate that the value is a `BigInt`.

Here's another example that shows the difference between a `Number` and a `BigInt`:

```
const a = Number.MAX_SAFE_INTEGER;
const b = BigInt(Number.MAX_SAFE_INTEGER);
console.log(a); // Logs "9007199254740991"
console.log(b); // Logs "9007199254740991n"
```

In the example above, the constant `a` is assigned the maximum safe integer value that a `Number` can represent, which is `9007199254740991`. The constant `b` is assigned the result of converting the maximum safe integer value represented as a `BigInt`, which is also `9007199254740991n`.

You can perform arithmetic operations with `BigInt` values just like with other numeric types. However, note that `BigInt` values cannot be mixed with `Number` values in arithmetic operations without explicit conversion. Also, some of the built-in JavaScript functions and methods may not yet support `BigInt` values.

Using `BigInt` is a good way to represent large integers that cannot be accurately represented with the `Number` type. It is recommended to use `BigInt` whenever you need to work with large integers in JavaScript.

String

The `String` type in JavaScript is used to represent sequences of characters, such as words, sentences, or entire pieces of text. Strings are written within quotes, either single quotes (`'`) or double quotes (`"`). For instance:

```
const name = "John Doe";
const message = 'Hello, world!';
```

In the example above, the constant `name` is assigned the string value `"John Doe"`, and the constant message is assigned the string value `'Hello, world!'`.

You can use the + operator to concatenate strings in JavaScript:

```
const firstName = "John";
const lastName = "Doe";
const fullName = firstName + " " + lastName;
console.log(fullName); // Logs "John Doe"
```

In the example above, the + operator is used to concatenate the values of `firstName`, `lastName`, and a space character into the string `"John Doe"`, which is assigned to the constant `fullName`.

There are also many built-in methods for working with strings in JavaScript, such as `.length` to get the length of a string, `.toUpperCase()` to convert a string to uppercase, `.toLowerCase()` to convert a string to lowercase, and many others. You can also use string methods such as `.slice()`, `.substring()`, `.substr()`, and `.indexOf()` to extract substrings or search for characters within a string.

Overall, the `String` type is an essential part of working with text data in JavaScript.

Null

The `null` value in JavaScript represents the intentional absence of any value. It is used to explicitly represent an "unknown" or "non-existent" value, for example when you want to indicate that an object property has no value. For instance:

```
const name = null;
console.log(name); // Logs "null"
```

In the example above, the constant `name` is assigned the value `null`, which represents the absence of a value.

It's important to note that `null` and `undefined` are not the same in JavaScript. `undefined` is a special value that indicates that a variable has been declared, but has not been assigned a value yet. On the other hand, `null` is explicitly assigned as a value, indicating that a value is intentionally unknown or non-existent.

Here's an example that demonstrates the difference between `null` and `undefined`:

```
let name;
console.log(name); // Logs "undefined"
```

```
name = null;
console.log(name); // Logs "null"
```

In the example above, the variable `name` is declared, but not assigned a value. When its value is logged, it returns `undefined`. Later, `name` is explicitly assigned the value `null`, and when its value is logged again, it returns `null`.

In summary, `null` is a value in JavaScript that represents the intentional absence of any value, while `undefined` indicates that a variable has been declared, but not assigned a value yet.

Function

The `Function` type in JavaScript represents a function or a block of code that can be executed when called. Functions are first-class citizens in JavaScript, which means that they can be assigned to variables, passed as arguments to other functions, and returned as values from other functions.

Functions in JavaScript can be declared using the `function` keyword, like this:

```javascript
function greet(name) {
  console.log("Hello, " + name + "!");
}

greet("John"); // logs "Hello, John!"
```

In the example above, the `greet` function takes a single argument `name` and logs a greeting to the console. The function is called with the argument `"John"`, which results in the string `"Hello, John!"` being logged into the console.

Functions in JavaScript can also be declared using function expressions, which are anonymous functions assigned to variables:

```
const square = function(x) {
  return x * x;
};

console.log(square(5)); // Logs 25
```

In the example above, the `square` function takes a single argument `x` and returns the square of `x`. The function is assigned to the `square` variable and can be called just like any other function.

Functions in JavaScript can also be declared using arrow functions, which are a shorthand for function expressions:

```
const square = x => x * x;

console.log(square(5)); // Logs 25
```

In the example above, the arrow function is equivalent to the function expression in the previous example. It takes a single argument `x` and returns the square of `x`. Arrow functions are shorter and more concise than function expressions, and are a popular way to declare simple functions in JavaScript.

Functions in JavaScript can have a return value, and they can be used to create closures, which are functions that have access to variables in their outer scope even after the outer function has returned.

Overall, the `Function` type in JavaScript is a powerful and flexible feature of the language and is widely used in web development to create reusable blocks of code that can be executed as needed.

Object

The `Object` type in JavaScript is a complex data structure that represents a collection of properties and values. An `Object` can be thought of as an unordered set of key-value pairs, where the keys are strings (or `Symbols`) and the values can be of any data type, including other objects.

Objects in JavaScript can be created using object literals, like this:

```
const person = {
  name: "John Doe",
  age: 30,
  address: {
    street: "123 Main St",
    city: "Anytown",
    state: "XX"
  }
};
```

In the example above, the `person` object has three properties: `name`, `age`, and `address`. The `address` property is itself an object with three properties.

Objects in JavaScript are dynamic, which means that properties can be added, modified, or deleted at any time. For instance:

```
const person = {
```

```
  name: "John Doe",
  age: 30,
  address: {
    street: "123 Main St",
    city: "Anytown",
    state: "XX"
  }
};

person.email = "john.doe@example.com";
delete person.address;
```

In the example above, a new property `email` is added to the `person` object, and the `address` property is deleted.

Objects in JavaScript also support inheritance, which means that objects can inherit properties and methods from their prototypes. For instance:

```
const animal = {
  makesSound: function() {
    console.log("Animal makes a sound");
  }
};

const dog = Object.create(animal);

dog.bark = function() {
  console.log("Woof!");
};
```

```
dog.makesSound(); // Logs "Animal makes a sound"
dog.bark(); // Logs "Woof!"
```

In the example above, the `animal` object is the prototype of the `dog` object, and the `dog` object inherits the `makesSound` method from the animal prototype.

Overall, the `Object` type in JavaScript is a versatile and powerful data structure that is widely used in web development. It provides a way to represent complex data structures and supports inheritance and dynamic property modification.

Symbol

The `Symbol` type in JavaScript is a new primitive data type introduced in ECMAScript 6 (ES6). A `Symbol` value is a unique, immutable identifier that can be used to create object properties that cannot be enumerated or overwritten.

A `Symbol` value is created using the `Symbol()` function, like this:

```
const mySymbol = Symbol();
```

You can also provide an optional string description to help identify the purpose of the symbol:

```
const mySymbol = Symbol("My Symbol");
```

`Symbols` are useful in a variety of situations, but are most commonly used as object property keys to prevent naming conflicts with other properties. For instance:

```
const person = {
  name: "John Doe",
```

```
    [Symbol("age")]: 30
};
```

In the example above, the `person` object has two properties: `name` and `Symbol("age")`. The `Symbol("age")` property is a unique identifier that cannot be overwritten by other properties with the same name, and it cannot be enumerated in a `for...in` loop (we will learn about loops in a later chapter) or with `Object.keys()` (we will learn more about this in a later chapter).

`Symbols` are also useful for creating unique object methods that cannot be overwritten by subclass prototypes.

Overall, `Symbols` are a useful addition to the JavaScript language, providing a way to create unique, immutable identifiers that can be used to create object properties with special properties and behaviors.

Date

The `Date` type in JavaScript represents a date and time value. Dates in JavaScript are represented as the number of milliseconds elapsed since January 1, 1970, 00:00:00 UTC. The `Date` type provides a number of methods for working with dates, such as getting the current date and time, formatting dates and times, and performing arithmetic on dates.

Here's an example of how to create a `Date` object and get the current date and time:

```
const now = new Date();
console.log(now); // Logs the current date and time
```

You can also create a `Date` object for a specific date and time using the `Date` constructor:

```
const birthday = new Date(1995, 11, 17);
console.log(birthday); // Logs "Thu Dec 14 1995 00:00:00
GMT-0700 (Central Europe Standard Time)"
```

In the example above, the `birthday` variable is assigned a `Date` object representing the date December 17, 1995.

The `Date` type provides methods for working with dates, such as getting the year, month, and day of the month, as well as the hours, minutes, and seconds:

```javascript
const now = new Date();
console.log(now.getFullYear()); // logs the current year
console.log(now.getMonth()); // logs the current month
(0-based, so 0 = January)
console.log(now.getDate()); // logs the current day of the
month
console.log(now.getHours()); // logs the current hour
console.log(now.getMinutes()); // logs the current minute
console.log(now.getSeconds()); // logs the current second
```

The `Date` type also provides methods for formatting dates as strings, such as `toLocaleDateString` and `toLocaleTimeString`:

```javascript
const now = new Date();
console.log(now.toLocaleDateString()); // logs the current
date, formatted for the user's locale
console.log(now.toLocaleTimeString()); // logs the current
time, formatted for the user's locale
```

Overall, the `Date` type in JavaScript is an essential part of working with dates and times in the language, and provides a number of methods for working with dates and times in a variety of formats.

Array

The `Array` type in JavaScript represents an ordered list of values. Arrays in JavaScript can hold any type of value, including numbers, strings, objects, and even other arrays.

Here's an example of how to create an array in JavaScript:

```
const fruits = ["apple", "banana", "cherry"];
console.log(fruits); // Logs ["apple", "banana", "cherry"]
```

You can access elements in an array using square brackets and an index, which starts at 0:

```
const firstFruit = fruits[0];
console.log(firstFruit); // Logs "apple"
```

Arrays in JavaScript are mutable, so you can change the values of elements in an array:

```
fruits[1] = "orange";
console.log(fruits); // Logs ["apple", "orange", "cherry"]
```

You can also add and remove elements from an array using the push and pop methods, respectively:

```
fruits.push("pear");
console.log(fruits); // Logs ["apple", "orange", "cherry",
"pear"]
fruits.pop();
console.log(fruits); // Logs ["apple", "orange", "cherry"]
```

The Array type in JavaScript provides many methods for working with arrays, such as map, filter, reduce, sort, and more. Here's an example of using the map method to create a new array with the length of each string in the fruits array, but don't worry if you don't fully understand it right now because we will take an in-depth look into arrays in a later chapter.

```
const fruitLengths = fruits.map(fruit => fruit.length);
console.log(fruitLengths); // Logs [5, 6, 6]
```

Overall, arrays in JavaScript are a powerful data structure that allows you to store and manipulate lists of values.

The String methods

Common string methods include `charAt`, `charCodeAt`, `concat`, `indexOf`, `lastIndexOf`, `match`, `replace`, `search`, `slice`, `split`, `substring`, `toLowerCase`, `toUpperCase`, `trim`, and `length`.

charAt

The `charAt()` is a method of the String object that returns the character at a specified index in a string.

For example, consider the following code:

```
const str = "Hello World";
const char = str.charAt(0);
```

The value of char will be `"H"`, which is the first character of the string `str`.

The index of the character to be returned is passed as an argument to the `charAt()` method. If the index is greater than or equal to the length of the string, the method returns an empty string. If the index is negative or non-integer, it will be rounded to the nearest integer before being used to retrieve a character.

charCodeAt

The `charCodeAt()` is a method of the String object that returns an integer representing the Unicode character code of the character at the specified index in the string.

```
const str = "Hello World";
const code = str.charCodeAt(0);
```

The value of `code` will be `72`, which is the Unicode character code for the letter `"H"`.

It's important to note that the `charCodeAt()` method returns a code in the range of `0` to `65535`, which represents the full range of Unicode characters. To get the full range of Unicode characters, use the `codePointAt()` method.

concat

The `concat()` method is a method of the `String` object that is used to concatenate two or more strings into a new string.

```
const str1 = "Hello";
const str2 = " World";
const result = str1.concat(str2);
```

In the example above, `str1` and `str2` are two strings, and the `concat()` method is used to combine them into a new string, `result`. The value of result will be "Hello World".

It's also possible to concatenate strings using the + operator in JavaScript.

```
var str1 = "Hello";
var str2 = " World";
var result = str1 + str2;
```

In the example above, `str1` and `str2` are combined into a new string result using the + operator. The value of `result` will be "Hello World".

indexOf

The `indexOf` method in JavaScript is a method of the `String` object that is used to search for a specified string value within another string and returns the index at which the first occurrence of the specified value can be found. If the specified value is not found, it returns `-1`.

Here's an example of how to use the `indexOf` method on a string:

```
const sentence = "The quick brown fox jumps over the lazy dog";
const index = sentence.indexOf("fox");
console.log(index); // Logs 16
```

In this example, the `indexOf` method searches the string `sentence` for the first occurrence of the string `"fox"` and returns the index `16`, which is the position of the first character of the match.

You can also pass a second argument to `indexOf` to specify the starting index from which the search should begin:

```
const index = sentence.indexOf("the", 10);
console.log(index); // Logs 25
```

In this example, the `indexOf` method starts the search from index `10` and returns the index of the first occurrence of `"the"` that appears after index `10`.

lastIndexOf

The `lastIndexOf` method in JavaScript is similar to the `indexOf` method, but it searches for the last occurrence of a specified string value within another string and returns the index of the last occurrence. If the specified value is not found, it returns `-1`.

Here's an example of how to use the `lastIndexOf` method on a string:

```
const sentence = "The quick brown fox jumps over the lazy dog";
const index = sentence.lastIndexOf("the");
console.log(index); // Logs 25
```

In this example, the `lastIndexOf` method searches the string sentence for the last occurrence of the string `"the"` and returns the index `25`, which is the position of the first character of the match.

You can also pass a second argument to `lastIndexOf` to specify the starting index from which the search should begin:

```
const index = sentence.lastIndexOf("the", 20);
console.log(index); // Logs 4
```

In this example, the `lastIndexOf` method starts the search from index 20 and returns the index of the last occurrence of `"the"` that appears before index 20.

match

The `match` method in JavaScript is a method of the `String` object that is used to search a string for a specified pattern and returns an array of all matches. If there are no matches, it returns `null`.

Here's an example of how to use the `match` method on a string:

```javascript
const sentence = "The quick brown fox jumps over the lazy dog";
const result = sentence.match(/the/gi);
console.log(result); // Logs [ 'The', 'the' ]
```

In this example, the `match` method searches the string `sentence` for all occurrences of the regular expression `/the/gi`, which matches the string `"the"` regardless of case, and returns an array of all matches.

You can also use the `match` method with a string as the pattern:

```javascript
const result = sentence.match("the");
console.log(result); // Logs ['The']
```

In this example, the `match` method searches the string `sentence` for the first occurrence of the string `"the"` and returns an array containing the match.

replace

The `replace` method in JavaScript is a method of the `String` object that is used to replace specified parts of a string with another string or a function.

Here's an example of how to use the `replace` method on a string:

```javascript
const sentence = "The quick brown fox jumps over the lazy dog";
const result = sentence.replace("the", "a");
console.log(result); // Logs "The quick brown fox jumps over a
lazy dog"
```

In this example, the replace method replaces the first occurrence of the string `"the"` in the string sentence with the string `"a"`.

You can also use a regular expression as the pattern:

```javascript
const result = sentence.replace(/the/gi, "a");
console.log(result); // Logs "a quick brown fox jumps over a
lazy dog"
```

In this example, the `replace` method replaces all occurrences of the regular expression /the/gi, which matches the string `"the"` regardless of case, with the string `"a"`.

You can also use a function as the replacement value:

```
const result = sentence.replace(/the/gi, function(match) {
  return match.toUpperCase();
});
console.log(result); // logs "THE quick brown fox jumps over
THE lazy dog"
```

In this example, the `replace` method replaces all occurrences of the regular expression /the/gi with the result of the function, which converts the matched string to uppercase.

replaceAll

The `replaceAll` method in JavaScript is similar to the `replace` method of the `String` object, but it replaces all occurrences of the specified pattern in the string, whereas `replace` only replaces the first occurrence.

Here's an example of how to use the `replaceAll` method on a string:

```javascript
const sentence = "the quick brown fox jumps over the lazy dog";
const result = sentence.replaceAll("the", "a");
console.log(result); // Logs "a quick brown fox jumps over a
lazy dog"
```

In this example, the `replaceAll` method replaces all occurrences of the string `"the"` in the string sentence with the string `"a"`.

search

The `search` method in JavaScript is a method of the `String` object that searches a string for a specified value and returns the position of the match. The method returns `-1` if no match is found.

Here's an example of how to use the `search` method on a string:

```
const sentence = "The quick brown fox jumps over the lazy dog";
const result = sentence.search("fox");
console.log(result); // Logs 16
```

In this example, the search method searches the string `sentence` for the first occurrence of the string `"fox"` and returns the position of the match, `16` in this case.

The `search` method can also accept a regular expression as the search value:

```
const result = sentence.search(/[A-Z]/);
console.log(result); // Logs 0
```

In this example, the `search` method searches the string `sentence` for the first occurrence of a capital letter (using a regular expression) and returns the position of the match, `0` in this case.

slice

The `slice` method in JavaScript is a method of the `String` object that returns a portion of a string. It takes two arguments, the start index and the end index, and returns a new string that includes the characters from the original string, starting from the start index up to, but not including, the end index.

Here's an example of how to use the `slice` method on a string:

```
const sentence = "The quick brown fox jumps over the lazy dog";
const result = sentence.slice(16, 19);
console.log(result); // Logs "fox"
```

In this example, the `slice` method extracts a portion of the string sentence starting from the 16th character and ending at the 19th character (not including the 19th character), and returns the new string `"fox"`.

If you only pass one argument to the `slice` method, it will extract all characters from that start index to the end of the string:

```
const result = sentence.slice(16);
console.log(result); // Logs "fox jumps over the lazy dog"
```

In this example, the `slice` method extracts a portion of the string sentence starting from the 16th character and ending at the end of the string, and returns the new string `"fox jumps over the lazy dog"`.

split

The `split` method in JavaScript is a method of the `String` object that splits a string into an array of substrings based on a specified separator. The separator can be a string or a regular expression.

Here's an example of how to use the `split` method on a string:

```javascript
const sentence = "The quick brown fox jumps over the lazy dog";
const result = sentence.split(" ");
console.log(result); // Logs ["The", "quick", "brown", "fox",
"jumps", "over", "the", "lazy", "dog"]
```

In this example, the `split` method splits the string sentence into an array of substrings, using a space character " " as the separator. The returned array contains 9 elements, each representing a word in the original string.

If you pass an empty string as a separator in the `split` method, it will split the string into an array of single-character substrings:

```javascript
const result = sentence.split("");
console.log(result); // Logs ["T", "h", "e", " ", "q", "u",
"i", "c", "k", " ", "b", "r", "o", "w", "n", " ", "f", "o",
"x", " ", "j", "u", "m", "p", "s", " ", "o", "v", "e", "r", "
", "t", "h", "e", " ", "l", "a", "z", "y", " ", "d", "o", "g"]
```

In this example, the `split` method splits the string `sentence` into an array of single-character substrings, using no separator. The returned array contains 43 elements, each representing a single character in the original string.

substring

The substring method in JavaScript is a method of the String object that returns a portion of a string. It takes two arguments: the starting index of the portion to extract, and the ending index of the portion to extract.

Here's an example of how to use the substring method on a string:

```
const sentence = "The quick brown fox jumps over the lazy dog";
const result = sentence.substring(4, 9);
console.log(result); // Logs "quick"
```

In this example, the substring method returns a portion of the string sentence, starting from the 4th character and ending at the 9th character. The returned value is the string "quick", which is the word starting from the 4th character and ending at the 9th character.

If you pass the end index argument that is smaller than the start index, substring will swap them:

```
const result = sentence.substring(9, 4);
console.log(result); // Logs "quick"
```

In this example, the `substring` method returns the same result as the previous example, even though the end index is smaller than the start index. This is because `substring` swaps the start and end indices to extract the portion of the string correctly.

If you only pass one argument to the substring method, it will extract all the characters from the specified starting index to the end of the string:

```
const result = sentence.substring(4);
console.log(result); // Logs "quick brown fox jumps over the
lazy dog"
```

In this example, the `substring` method returns a portion of the string `sentence`, starting from the 4th character and extracting all the characters until the end of the string. The returned value is the string "quick brown fox jumps over the lazy dog", which is the portion of the original string starting from the 4th character.

toLowerCase

The `toLowerCase` method in JavaScript is a method of the `String` object that returns a new string with all the characters in lowercase.

Here's an example of how to use the `toLowerCase` method on a string:

```
const sentence = "The Quick Brown Fox Jumps Over The Lazy Dog";
const result = sentence.toLowerCase();
console.log(result); // logs "the quick brown fox jumps over
the lazy dog"
```

In this example, the `toLowerCase` method returns a new string with all the characters in the original string sentence in lowercase. The returned value is the string `"the quick brown fox jumps over the lazy dog"`, which is the original string with all the characters in lowercase.

Note that the original string `sentence` is not modified by the `toLowerCase` method. The method returns a new string with lowercase characters, but the original string remains unchanged.

toUpperCase

The `toUpperCase` method in JavaScript is a method of the `String` object that returns a new string with all the characters in uppercase.

Here's an example of how to use the `toUpperCase` method on a string:

```
const sentence = "The Quick Brown Fox Jumps Over The Lazy Dog";
const result = sentence.toUpperCase();
console.log(result); // Logs "THE QUICK BROWN FOX JUMPS OVER
THE LAZY DOG"
```

In this example, the `toUpperCase` method returns a new string with all the characters in the original string `sentence` in uppercase. The returned value is the string `"THE QUICK BROWN FOX JUMPS OVER THE LAZY DOG"`, which is the original string with all the characters in uppercase.

Note that the original string `sentence` is not modified by the `toUpperCase` method. The method returns a new string with uppercase characters, but the original string remains unchanged.

trim

The `trim` method in JavaScript is a method of the `String` object that returns a new string with whitespace characters removed from the beginning and end of the string.

Here's an example of how to use the `trim` method on a string:

```
const sentence = "  The Quick Brown Fox Jumps Over The Lazy Dog ";
const result = sentence.trim();
console.log(result); // logs "The Quick Brown Fox Jumps Over The Lazy Dog"
```

In this example, the `trim` method returns a new string with the whitespace characters at the beginning and end of the original string `sentence` removed. The returned value is the string `"The Quick Brown Fox Jumps Over The Lazy Dog"`, which is the original string with the whitespace characters removed from the beginning and end.

Note that the original string `sentence` is not modified by the `trim` method. The method returns a new string with the whitespace characters removed, but the original string remains unchanged.

length

The `length` property in JavaScript is a property of the `String` object that returns the length of the string, measured in characters.

Here's an example of how to use the `length` property on a string:

```javascript
const sentence = "The Quick Brown Fox Jumps Over The Lazy Dog";
const result = sentence.length;
console.log(result); // Logs 43
```

In this example, the `length` property returns the value `43`, which is the number of characters in the string `sentence`. The `length` property is often used to determine the number of characters in a string or to loop through all characters in a string.

Note that the `length` property is read-only, meaning that you cannot set or modify its value. You can only access its value to retrieve the length of the string.

Arithmetic operations

JavaScript supports a variety of arithmetic operations, including addition, subtraction, multiplication, division, modulo, and others. These operations can be performed on `Number` objects as well as `BigInt`.

Here are some examples of arithmetic operations in JavaScript:

```javascript
const a = 10;
const b = 5;
```

```javascript
const addition = a + b;
console.log(addition); // Logs 15

const subtraction = a - b;
console.log(subtraction); // Logs 5

const multiplication = a * b;
console.log(multiplication); // Logs 50
const division = a / b;
console.log(division); // Logs 2

const modulo = a % b;
console.log(modulo); // Logs 0

const exponential = a ** b;
console.log(exponential); // Logs 100000
```

In this example, the + operator is used for addition, the - operator is used for subtraction, the * operator is used for multiplication, the / operator is used for division, the % operator is used for modulo, and the ** operator is used for exponential calculations. These operators allow you to perform arithmetic operations in JavaScript and manipulate numbers as needed.

The Math object

The `Math` object in JavaScript is a built-in object that provides a variety of mathematical functions and properties. You can use the `Math` object to perform complex mathematical operations and calculations in your JavaScript programs.

Here are a few examples of the functions available in the `Math` object:

```
const pi = Math.PI;
console.log(pi); // logs 3.141592653589793
```

```javascript
const e = Math.E;
console.log(e); // logs 2.718281828459045

const absolute = Math.abs(-10);
console.log(absolute); // logs 10

const ceil = Math.ceil(10.1);
console.log(ceil); // logs 11

const floor = Math.floor(10.9);
console.log(floor); // logs 10

const round = Math.round(10.5);
console.log(round); // logs 11

const max = Math.max(10, 20, 30);
console.log(max); // logs 30

const min = Math.min(10, 20, 30);
console.log(min); // logs 10

const power = Math.pow(2, 3);
console.log(power); // logs 8

const squareRoot = Math.sqrt(16);
console.log(squareRoot); // logs 4

const random = Math.random();
console.log(random); // logs a random number between 0 and 1
```

In this example, the `Math.PI` property returns the value of pi, the `Math.E` property returns the value of the mathematical constant e, the `Math.abs()` function returns the absolute value of a number, the `Math.ceil()` function returns the smallest integer greater than or equal to a number, the `Math.floor()` function returns the largest integer less than or equal to a number, the `Math.round()` function rounds a number to the nearest integer, the `Math.max()` function returns the largest number from a list of numbers, the `Math.min()` function returns the smallest number from a list of numbers, the `Math.pow()` function returns the value of a number raised to a power, the `Math.sqrt()` function returns the square root of a number, and the `Math.random()` function returns a random number between 0 and 1. The `Math` object is a powerful tool for performing mathematical operations in JavaScript.

Math.abs

In JavaScript, the `Math.abs` function returns the absolute value of a number. Absolute value is the distance of a number from 0, and it is always positive. The syntax for using `Math.abs` is `Math.abs(number)` where number is the value whose absolute value you want to determine. For instance:

```
const x = -10;
console.log(Math.abs(x)); // Output: 10
```

Math.abs can be used to remove the sign of a number, making it positive, regardless of its original sign.

Math.ceil

In JavaScript, the Math.ceil function returns the smallest integer that is greater than or equal to a given number. The syntax for using Math.ceil is `Math.ceil(number)` where number is the value you want to round up. For instance:

```
const x = 3.14;
console.log(Math.ceil(x)); // Output: 4
```

`Math.ceil` is useful for rounding numbers up to the next whole number when dealing with calculations.

Math.floor

In JavaScript, the `Math.floor` function returns the largest integer that is less than or equal to a given number. The syntax for using Math.floor is `Math.floor(number)` where number is the value you want to round down. For instance:

```javascript
const x = 3.14;
console.log(Math.floor(x)); // Output: 3
```

`Math.floor` is useful for rounding numbers down to the previous whole number when dealing with calculations.

Math.round

In JavaScript, the `Math.round` function returns the nearest integer to a given number. The syntax for using Math.round is `Math.round(number)` where number is the value you want to round. For instance:

```
const x = 3.14;
console.log(Math.round(x)); // Output: 3
```

`Math.round` uses the standard rounding rules where values with a fractional part of exactly 0.5 are rounded to the nearest even integer. For example:

```
const x = 3.5;
console.log(Math.round(x)); // Output: 4
```

`Math.round` is useful for rounding numbers to the nearest whole number when dealing with calculations.

Math.max

`Math.max` is a method in JavaScript that returns the largest number of a set of numbers. The syntax for using Math.max is `Math.max(number1, number2, numberX)` where `number1`, `number2`, `numberX` are the values you want to find the maximum of. If any of the parameters is not a number, the function returns `NaN`. For instance:

```
const a = Math.max(1, 2, 3); // 3
const b = Math.max(4, 2, 7, 5); // 7
const c = Math.max(1, "hello"); // NaN
```

You can pass an unlimited number of arguments to `Math.max` to find the largest of all the values. If no arguments are passed or if one of the arguments is not a number, `Math.max` will return `-Infinity`. For instance:

```
console.log(Math.max()); // Output: -Infinity
```

`Math.max` is useful for finding the maximum value in a set of numbers, which can be useful in many mathematical calculations or when processing data in an array.

Math.min

`Math.min` is a method in JavaScript that returns the lowest value from a list of arguments or numbers. The method takes in an arbitrary number of parameters and returns the smallest number among them. If any of the parameters is not a number, the function returns `NaN`. For instance:

```
const a = Math.min(1, 2, 3); // 1
const b = Math.min(4, 2, 7, 5); // 2
const c = Math.min(1, "hello"); // NaN
```

You can pass an unlimited number of arguments to `Math.min` to find the lowest of all the values. If no arguments are passed or if one of the arguments is not a number, `Math.min` will return `Infinity`. For instance:

```
console.log(Math.max()); // Output: Infinity
```

Math.pow

`Math.pow` is a method in JavaScript that returns the value of a number raised to a specified power. It takes two parameters: the base number and the exponent.

```javascript
const a = Math.pow(2, 3); // 8
const b = Math.pow(10, 2); // 100
const c = Math.pow(5, 0.5); // 2.23606797749979
```

Math.sqrt

`Math.sqrt` is a method in JavaScript that returns the square root of a given number. It takes a single parameter, which is the number you want to find the square root of.

```
const a = Math.sqrt(9);  // 3
const b = Math.sqrt(16); // 4
const c = Math.sqrt(2);  // 1.4142135623730951
```

Math.random

`Math.random` is a method in JavaScript that returns a random number between 0 (inclusive) and 1 (exclusive). It doesn't take any parameters.

It's commonly used to generate random numbers for various purposes, such as generating random numbers for game programming, simulations, etc. For instance:

```
const randomNumber = Math.random(); // returns a random number
between 0 (inclusive) and 1 (exclusive)
```

You can use `Math.random` along with other mathematical operations to generate random numbers within a specific range:

```
const randomNumberBetween1And10 = Math.floor(Math.random() *
10) + 1;
```

In the example above, we're using `Math.floor` to round to number to the lowest integer and we're using `Math.random` to generate a number between 0 (inclusive) and 1 (exclusive) and multiplying that value by 10 as it's the maximum value that we would like to generate, after those operations happen, we are adding the minimum value that we would like to be generated, in this case 1.

Conditional statements

Conditional statements in JavaScript allow you to execute a certain piece of code only if a certain condition is met. There are three main types of conditional statements: `if`, `else`, and `switch`

The `if` statement

The `if` statement in JavaScript allows you to execute a block of code only if a specified condition is true. The basic syntax of the if statement is as follows:

```
if (condition) {
    // code to be executed if condition is true
}
```

For instance:

```
const score = 70;

if (score >= 50) {
    console.log("You passed the test!");
}
```

In this example, the code inside the `if` statement will only be executed if the value of `score` is greater than or equal to `50`.

You can also use the `else` statement to execute a different block of code if the condition is false:

```
const score = 40;

if (score >= 50) {
  console.log("You passed the test!");
} else {
  console.log("You failed the test.");
}
```

In this example, if the value of `score` is greater than or equal to 50, the first code block will be executed and the message `"You passed the test!"` will be logged to the console. If the condition is false, the code inside the else statement will be executed and the message `"You failed the test."` will be logged to the console.

You can also use multiple `if` and `else if` statements to evaluate multiple conditions:

```
const score = 70;

if (score >= 90) {
  console.log("You got an A!");
} else if (score >= 80) {
  console.log("You got a B.");
} else if (score >= 70) {
```

```
  console.log("You got a C.");
} else {
  console.log("You got a D or lower.");
}
```

In this example, the first condition if (score >= 90) is evaluated first. If the condition is true, the code inside the first if statement will be executed and the message "You got an A!" will be logged to the console. If the first condition is false, the next else if condition will be evaluated, and so on. If none of the conditions are true, the code inside the else statement will be executed.

The `switch` statement

The `switch` statement in JavaScript is a type of conditional statement that tests the value of an expression against a set of possible cases, and executes the code associated with the first matching case. It provides a convenient way to handle multiple cases based on a single expression.

Here's an example of how to use the `switch` statement:

```
switch (expression) {
  case value1:
    // code to be executed if expression matches value1
    break;
  case value2:
    // code to be executed if expression matches value2
    break;
  ...
  case valueN:
    // code to be executed if expression matches valueN
    break;
  default:
    // code to be executed if no match is found
}
```

Here's a simple example that uses the `switch` statement to choose which message to display based on the day of the week:

```javascript
let day = new Date().getDay(); // 0-based day of the week

switch (day) {
  case 0:
    console.log("Sunday");
    break;
  case 1:
    console.log("Monday");
    break;
  case 2:
    console.log("Tuesday");
    break;
  case 3:
    console.log("Wednesday");
    break;
  case 4:
    console.log("Thursday");
    break;
  case 5:
    console.log("Friday");
    break;
  case 6:
    console.log("Saturday");
    break;
  default:
    console.log("Invalid Day");
}
```

The `switch` statement is especially useful when you want to perform a specific action based on multiple values of a single expression, rather than using a series of `if...else` statements, which can quickly become complex and difficult to read. The use cases of the `switch` statement can range from simple data type comparisons to more complex logic that can handle multiple conditions.

Arrays in JavaScript

An `Array` in JavaScript is a global object used in the construction of lists.

The prototype, or the core functionality of the `Array`, includes methods to perform reading, writing, listing, and mutation of the elements within the list. An array's type and length can change at any time and the data can be stored in non-contiguous positions.

Arrays in JavaScript are zero-indexed, meaning that the first position of an array is always zero.

Creating an array

Creating an array with JavaScript takes little effort.

```
const people = ['Alex', 'Daniel', 'Rafael', 'May'];
```

The `people` variable now holds an array with 4 elements of type `String` within it, indexed as follows:

```
0. Alex
1. Daniel
2. Rafael
3. May
```

As you can see, the first position of the array, index zero, corresponds to the string `Alex`. The length of this array is four.

If you would like to create an empty array instead, you will have to:

```
const people = [];
```

This will create an empty array and the length of it would be zero.

Getting an array's length

To get an array's length you can use the `length` property:

```javascript
const people = ['Alex', 'Daniel', 'Jake', 'May'];
people.length; // 4
```

Accessing an element by its index

In order to access an element within an array by its index, we should do as follows:

```
const people = ['Alex', 'Daniel', 'Jake', 'May'];
people[1]; // Daniel
```

If you try to access an element by its index and there's no element at the given index, you will get undefined in return.

```
const people = ['Alex', 'Daniel', 'Jake', 'May'];
people[4]; // undefined
```

If you have a dynamic array and you want to access the last element in the array, you can use the length property to get the number of elements in the array and subtract 1, because if you remember, arrays are zero-indexed, that's why we need to subtract 1 from the length of the array.

```
const people = ['Alex', 'Daniel', 'Jake', 'May'];
people[people.length - 1]; // May
```

Let's see what happens if you don't subtract 1 from the `people.length` property.

```
const people = ['Alex', 'Daniel', 'Jake', 'May'];
people[people.length]; // undefined
```

`people.length` will return 4 and the 4th position of the `people` array is, in fact, `undefined`.

for loop

A `for` loop in JavaScript is a control flow statement that allows you to execute a block of code repeatedly, a specified number of times, or until a certain condition is met.

First, we should create an array and get the length of it.

```javascript
const people = ['Alex', 'Daniel', 'Jake', 'May'];
const amountOfPeople = people.length; // 4;
```

Now we need to construct the `for` loop. This is one of the most basic things you will learn when studying computer science.

```javascript
for (let index = 0; index <= amountOfPeople - 1; index++) {}
```

Let's take a look at the signature of a `for` loop.

- **for**: this is a reserved word in JavaScript used to declare a **for** loop.
- **let** index = 0: this is a variable declaration and it's going to be used to hold the current iteration index.

- index <= amountOfPeople - 1: this is the predicate used to determine if the loop should keep being executed or finish the iterations, if the predicate is equal to true it will continue executing, if the predicate is equal to false it will finish executing.
- index++: this is the action that will be executed when an iteration finishes, commonly, you use this to increase the `indexing` variable by one or by any number that you'd like to.

Now let's glue it all together to construct a for loop that will display all of the persons' names in the console.

```
const people = ['Alex', 'Daniel', 'Jake', 'May'];
const amountOfPeople = people.length; // 4;

for (let index = 0; index <= amountOfPeople - 1; index++) {
  console.log(people[index]);
}
```

If you execute this code in your Node terminal or in a REPL, you should see an output like the following:

```
Alex
Daniel
Jake
May
```

forEach loop

Iterating an array with a `forEach` callback is not as efficient as the `for loop` when you need to iterate over a large array but someone could say that it's more visually appealing and readable, if performance is not important and you're aiming for readability, then you should go with `forEach`. But remember, that the `forEach` callback function cannot be `asynchronous` (we will take a look into this in a later chapter) and if you try to **async/await** it, it will definitely give you more than one or two headaches.

Let's take a look at how to use the `forEach` callback function

```
const people = ['Alex', 'Daniel', 'Jake', 'May'];

people.forEach(function (element, index, array) {
  console.log(element);
});
```

Now let's take a look at the signature of a `forEach` callback function as we did with the **for** loop.

1. `people.forEach()`: as we can see here, the `.forEach()` is a method from the `Array` prototype (core functionality) and it's available to you because the `people` variable is an `Array` object.

2. **function**(element, index, array): this is the callback function that will be called for each of the elements within the array. This function will get 3 parameters passed along for you to make use of them, these parameters are:
   a. element: the current element of the array in this iteration.
   b. index: the current index of this iteration.
   c. array: the whole array will be passed to this property just in case you'd need to access it for something.

It might be a little more readable than the `for loop` but if performance is not important, feel free to depend on it as needed. You can even make it shorter with an `arrow function` with implicit return:

```
const people = ['Alex', 'Daniel', 'Jake', 'May'];
people.forEach((element, index, array) =>
console.log(element));
```

IIterating over an array with a for...of loop

Another way for iterating over an array is with a **for of** loop, this is a very simple and readable loop type.

Let's iterate over the fruits on the fridge!

```javascript
const fridge = [
  { fruit: '🍎', amount: 2 },
  { fruit: '🍎', amount: 4 },
  { fruit: '🍐', amount: 1 },
  { fruit: '🥝', amount: 0 },
  { fruit: '🍌', amount: 3 }
];

for (let fruit of fridge) {
  console.log(fruit);
}

// {fruit: "🍎", amount: 2}
// {fruit: "🍎", amount: 4}
// {fruit: "🍐", amount: 1}
// {fruit: "🥝", amount: 0}
// {fruit: "🍌", amount: 3}
```

As we can see from the code snippet above, this is a much simpler way to iterate over an array. For each of the iterations, it stores the value of the current index element on the `fruit` variable and you can use it to manipulate it as you would like.

Adding elements to an array

In order to add elements to an array we have multiple ways, we can `push` an element into the last position, we can store an element in a specific array's position based on an index or we can `unshift` an element into the first position of the array. Let's take a look at some of those methods for adding elements to an array.

push elements into an array

We are going to use the `push()` method from the `Array` object to add an element to the end of an array. Let's say we have an array of fruits that contains an apple 🍎, a pear 🍐, and a lemon 🍋, and we did some groceries and we would like to add a banana too 🍌, we don't care where to put it, so we're just going to `push` it in the end.

```
let fruit = ['🍎', '🍐', '🍋'];
fruit.push('🍌');
```

The `fruit` array will now contain an apple 🍎, a pear 🍐, a lemon 🍋 and a banana 🍌.

📣 Heads up! The `push` method mutates the original array and this could lead to bugs in your code. You should try to achieve immutability in your code to easily identify bugs.

Storing elements based on an index position

We're going to use the `index` position of an array to store the watermelon 🍉 we just bought into a specific place in the `fruit` array that we previously created.

```
let fruit = ['🍎', '🍐', '🍋', '🍌'];
fruit[4] = '🍉';
```

The `fruit` array will now contain an apple 🍎, a pear 🍐, a lemon 🍋, a banana 🍌 and, in the 4th position of the array, a watermelon 🍉.

Let's imagine that we have purchased the watermelon 🍉 but we don't have any more space in the fridge so we need to take out fruit in order to store the watermelon 🍉. How do we do this? Let's assume we don't want any more lemons 🍋.

```
let fruit = ['🍎', '🍐', '🍋', '🍌'];

fruit[2] = '🍉';
```

After this change, the `fruit` array will now contain an apple 🍎, a pear 🍐, a watermelon 🍉 and a banana 🍌. The lemon 🍋 is gone because we have used its `index` position to tell the array that in that particular position we would like to have a watermelon 🍉 instead of a lemon 🍋.

unshift elements into an array

We are going to use the unshift() method from the Array object to add an element to the beginning of the array. Let's say we still have this fruit array but we want to add more fruit to it because we have purchased a new fruit, an orange 🍊, and we would like to save it for the last because it's the newest fruit and you should always it the fruit that you've purchased before the new fruit.

```
let fruit = ['🍎', '🍐', '🍉', '🍌'];

fruit.unshift('🍊');
```

The fruit array will now contain an orange 🍊, an apple 🍎, a pear 🍐, a watermelon 🍉 and a banana 🍌.

📢 Heads up! The unshift method mutates the original array and this could lead to bugs in your code. You should try to achieve immutability in your code to easily identify bugs.

Removing elements from an array

We are going to use the `pop()` method from the `Array` object to remove the last element from an array. Let's say we still have this fruit array and we want to eat some fruit but would like to eat the ones we purchased recently (not a good idea with fruit!).

```
let fruit = ['🍊', '🍎', '🍐', '🍉', '🍌'];

fruit.pop();
```

The `fruit` array will now contain an orange 🍊, an apple 🍎, a pear 🍐 and a watermelon 🍉, but the banana will be gone because we have just eaten it.

📣 Heads up! The `pop` method mutates the original array and this could lead to bugs in your code. You should try to achieve immutability in your code to easily identify bugs.

Removing various elements by position

With the splice(**from,** amount) method from the Array object we can remove a subset of the elements on the array by an index range. We provide the **from** index where the subtraction will start and the amount of elements that we would like to subtract from the starting point.

```
let fruit = ['🍎', '🍎', '🍐', '🥝', '🍌'];

let removedElements = fruit.splice(1, 3); // ['🍎', '🍐', '🥝']

fruit; // ['🍎', '🍌'];
```

The splice method takes out the given elements and returns them so you can use them separately as a new array.

📢 Heads up! The splice method mutates the original array and this could lead to bugs in your code. You should try to achieve immutability in your code to easily identify bugs.

Finding the index of an element in an array

Imagine that you want to know where the apples 🍎 are located in your fridge, how would you do this? Thankfully, the `Array` object has a very handy method to tell you the index of an element within an array, that method is `indexOf`, and given an element, it will return you the index of that element within the array or `-1` if the element is not found in the array.

```
const fruit = ['🍎', '🍎', '🍐', '🍉', '🍌'];

const appleIndex = fruits.indexOf('🍎'); // 1
```

Now we want to find where the watermelon 🍉 is at!

```
const fruit = ['🍎', '🍎', '🍐', '🍉', '🍌'];

const watermelonIndex = fruits.indexOf('🍉'); // 3
```

Do we have any lemons 🍋?

```
const fruit = ['🍎', '🍎', '🍐', '🍉', '🍌'];
```

```
const lemonIndex = fruits.indexOf('🍋'); // -1
```

We don't have any lemons 🍋 on the fridge and that's why the `lemonIndex` variable will hold a `-1`.

> 📢 Heads up! The `indexOf` method will return the `index` of **the first element** that matches within the array. If you have various elements that are the same, the `index` that will be returned will be the one that matches first from index 0 to index n.

Another way of finding the index of an element in an array

Imagine that you know you have an apple 🍎 but you don't actually know where it's located on the fridge. How would you do this? Thankfully, we have the `findIndex(predicate)` method in the `Array` object that will allow us to obtain the index in the array of a given element. This method takes a callback function as the main and only argument as a predicate to check for the element that we would like to obtain its index and returns the index of the matching element or `-1` if the element is not found in the array.

```
const fruit = ['🍅', '🍎', '🍐', '🍋', '🍌'];

const appleIndex = fruits.findIndex('🍎'); // 1
```

Where are the lemons 🍋 in our fridge?

```
const fruit = ['🍅', '🍎', '🍐', '🍋', '🍌'];

const lemonIndex = fruits.findIndex('🍋'); // -1
```

♠ Heads up! The `findIndex` method will return the `index` of **the first element** that matches within the array. If you have various elements that are the same, the `index` that will be returned will be the one that matches first from index 0 to index n.

Copying an array

Copying arrays is a common use case in many applications and scenarios. Copying arrays is a simple task that can be done in different ways. We can use the `slice()` method from the `Array` object to create a copy of the array into a new variable, or we can use the `spread operator (...)` feature to create a copy of the array into a new variable.

Using slice to copy an array

We can use the `slice` method to duplicate the array. This method doesn't mutate the original array so it's kept intact and therefore, it's immutable and better for avoiding bugs 🐛

```
const basketOne = ['🍎', '🍏', '🍐', '🍈', '🍌'];
const basketTwo = basketOne.slice();

basketOne; // ['🍎', '🍏', '🍐', '🍈', '🍌']
basketTwo; // ['🍎', '🍏', '🍐', '🍈', '🍌']
```

Using slice to copy a part of the array

We can use the `slice(start, end)` method to copy a section of the array from the start point (inclusive) to the ending index (exclusive). This method doesn't mutate the original array so it's kept intact and therefore, it's immutable and better for avoiding bugs 🐞

```
const basketOne = ['🍎', '🍎', '🍐', '🍅', '🍌'];
const basketTwo = basketOne.slice(1, 3);

basketOne; // ['🍎', '🍎', '🍐', '🍅', '🍌']
basketTwo; // ['🍎', '🍐']
```

Using the spread operator to copy an array

We can use the `spread operator (...)` to duplicate an array. This method also doesn't mutate the original array so it's kept intact and therefore, it's immutable and better for avoiding bugs 🐞

```
const basketOne = ['🍎', '🍎', '🍐', '🍋', '🍌'];
const basketTwo = [...basketOne];

basketOne; // ['🍎', '🍎', '🍐', '🍋', '🍌']
basketTwo; // ['🍎', '🍎', '🍐', '🍋', '🍌']
```

As you can see both of the options are equal in the result and doesn't differ in performance so it's up to you to decide which one you'd like to use.

Concatenating arrays with concat

We can use the `concat(Array)` method to concatenate multiple arrays together so we can obtain an array that will be the combination (concatenation) of other arrays. This method doesn't mutate any of the original arrays so it's kept intact and therefore, it's immutable and better for avoiding bugs 🐞

```
const basketOne = ['🍎', '🍏'];
const basketTwo = ['🍐', '🥝', '🍌'];

const combinedBasket = basketOne.concat(basketTwo);
```

After using the `.concat(array)` method on an array and passing the array that will be concatenated, it will return a new array instead of modifying the original array. This way, the `combinedBasket` will contain the following items: '🍎', '🍏', '🍐', '🥝', '🍌', and the `basketOne` and `basketTwo` will remain intact.

Concatenating arrays with the spread operator

We can use the spread operator (...) to concatenate multiple arrays together so we can obtain an array that will be the combination (concatenation) of other arrays. This method doesn't mutate any of the original arrays so it's kept intact and therefore, it's immutable and better for avoiding bugs 🐞

```
const basketOne = ['🍎', '🍏'];
const basketTwo = ['🍐', '🍊', '🍌'];

const combinedBasket = [...basketOne, ...basketTwo];
```

After using the spread operator (...) on an array and spreading both arrays into a new array will make the same effect as using the .concat(array) method. Remember that spreading an array will not modify the original array. This way, the combinedBasket will contain the following items: '🍎', '🍏', '🍐', '🍊', '🍌', and the basketOne and basketTwo will remain intact.

Finding an element in the array

With the `find(predicate)` method from the `Array` object we can find the first element that matches the predicate that we pass as the argument to the `find` function. If none of the elements on the array matches the predicate, `undefined` will be returned from the `find` function.

```
const basket = ['🍏', '🍎', '🍐', '🍉', '🍌'];

const watermelon = basket.find(function (element) {
  return element === '🍉';
});

watermelon; // 🍉
```

```
const basket = ['🍏', '🍎', '🍐', '🍉', '🍌'];

const lemon = basket.find(function (element) {
  return element === '🍋';
});

lemon; // undefined
```

We can make this even shorter with `arrow functions` with implicit returns!

```javascript
const basket = ['🍎', '🍏', '🍐', '🥝', '🍌'];

const watermelon = basket.find((element) => element === '🥝');

watermelon; // 🥝


const basket = ['🍎', '🍏', '🍐', '🥝', '🍌'];

const lemon = basket.find((element) => element === '🍋');

lemon; // undefined
```

Checking some elements in the array

With the `some(predicate)` method from the `Array` object we can determine if some of the elements in the array match the given predicate. This method returns `true` or `false` depending if there are elements that match the predicate or not. This method also returns `false` for any predicate on an empty array.

Let's imagine we want to check if we have some apples 🍎 in our fridge. How do we do this?

```
const fridge = ['🍎', '🍎', '🍐', '🍋', '🍌'];

const fridgeHasApples = fridge.some(function (element) {
  return element === '🍎';
});

fridgeHasApples; // true
```

Let's check if our fridge also has some lemons 🍋 in it!

```
const fridge = ['🍎', '🍎', '🍐', '🍋', '🍌'];

const fridgeHasLemons = fridge.some(function (element) {
```

```
    return element === '🍋';
});

fridgeHasLemons; // false
```

Uh oh! We need to do some groceries because we ran out of lemons 🍋!

Checking every element in the array

With the `every(predicate)` method from the `Array` object we can determine if every one of the elements in the array matches the given predicate. This method returns `true` or `false` depending if all of the elements match the predicate or not. This method also returns `true` for any predicate on an empty array.

Let's imagine we want to check if all of the fruit we have in the fridge are apples 🍎. How do we do this?

```
const fridge = ['🍎', '🍎', '🍎', '🍎', '🍎'];

const everythingIsApple = fridge.every(function (element) {
  return element === '🍎';
});

everythingIsApple; // true
```

Let's check in a fridge with more fruit diversity!

```
const fridge = ['🍎', '🍎', '🍐', '🥝', '🍌'];

const everythingIsApple = fridge.every(function (element) {
```

```
  return element === '🍎';
});

everythingIsApple; // false
```

Using fill to change elements in an array

With the `fill(element, from, to)` method from the `Array` object we can change values within an array.

Let's try to fill our fridge with apples 🍎!

```
const fridge = ['', '', '', '', ''];

fridge.fill('🍎');

fridge; // ['🍎', '🍎', '🍎', '🍎', '🍎']
```

Now let's try to fill the fridge with some pears 🍐 but just in the spaces 2 to 4 in the fridge!

```
const fridge = ['🍎', '', '', '', '🍎'];

fridge.fill('🍐', 1, 3);

fridge; // ['🍎', '🍐', '🍐', '🍐', '🍎']
```

There are some interesting things you should know about the `fill` method:

- If **from** is not used, it will be 0 (zero) by default.
- If **from** is negative, it will be calculated as `array.length + from`.
- If **to** is not used, it will use the `array.length` by default.
- If **to** is negative, it will be calculated as `array.length - to`.
- The `fill` method mutates the array should be used carefully so it won't introduce bugs 🐛.
- If the `element` is an object, it will copy its reference and fill the array with references to it.

Sorting elements in an array

With the sort(**function**(a, b)) method from the Array object we can sort the elements within the array. If you don't pass a sorting function as the main and only argument to the sort method, it will use the string value based on its Unicode position. This method mutates the original array and should be used carefully so it won't introduce bugs 🐛.

```
const numbers = [4, 2, 3, 5, 1, 6, 9];

numbers.sort(); // [1, 2, 3, 4, 5, 6, 9]
```

Let's look at another example but this time the array will contain strings.

```
const fruit = ['bananas', 'lemons', 'apples'];

fruit.sort(); // ["apples", "bananas", "lemons"]
```

Now we're going to introduce our own compare **function** so we can make the sort method behave like we want. Let's imagine we have an array with posts, which are objects with the following shape:

```
const post = {
  title: 'Hello there',
  createdAt: new Date('03/23/2021'),
  content: '...'
};


let posts = [
  { title: 'Hello 3', createdAt: new Date('05/23/2021') },
  { title: 'Hello 2', createdAt: new Date('04/23/2021') },
  { title: 'Hello 4', createdAt: new Date('06/23/2021') },
  { title: 'Hello 1', createdAt: new Date('03/23/2021') },
];

posts.sort(function (postA, postB) {
  if (postA.createdAt.getTime() === postB.createdAt.getTime())
return 0;
  if (postA.createdAt.getTime() > postB.createdAt.getTime())
return -1;
  if (postA.createdAt.getTime() < postB.createdAt.getTime())
return 1;
});
```

We have implemented a sorting function to sort the posts by the createdAt property, and because that property contains a Date object, we can use the getTime function of it to retrieve the number of milliseconds elapsed since the Unix Time (January 1st, 1970), then we use this numbers to compare which one is bigger. The sorting function expects you to return a number in a specific way:

- If the compare function returns a number less than 0, it places the postA in a lower index than postB.
- If the compare function returns a number greater than 0, it places the postB in a lower index than postA.
- If the compare function returns 0, it won't change postA or postB indexes.
- The compare function always needs to return the same value given a specific pair of elements a and b as well as their arguments.

By knowing this, you can sort the array in any manner you'd like to. In the example above, we're reversing the -1 and 1 and by doing so, we're sorting the array in a descending way.

📢 Heads up! The splice method mutates the original array and this could lead to bugs in your code. You should try to achieve immutability in your code to easily identify bugs.

Map (iterate) over the elements in the array

With the map(**function**(element, index)) method from the Array object
we can iterate over the elements and apply the result of the function call
to each of the elements and return a new array with the results.

Let's imagine we have a basket of fruits, but this time, each of the fruits is
gonna be a JavaScript object like the following:

```
const fruitObject = {
    fruit: '🍎',
    amount: 1
};
```

The fruitObject will contain two properties, one called fruit that will
contain the fruit itself and an amount property that will contain how many
of this fruit we have. In the above example, we have one (amount: 1) apple
(fruit: '🍎').

Let's fill the fridge with fruit!

```
const fridge = [
    { fruit: '🍎', amount: 1 },
```

```
  { fruit: '🍎', amount: 1 },
  { fruit: '🍐', amount: 1 },
  { fruit: '🍌', amount: 1 },
  { fruit: '🍌', amount: 1 }
];
```

Now that we have the fridge full of tasty and juicy fruit let's do some groceries because you should always try to have your fridge full of healthy fruit. We need to consider that we don't have enough room in our fridge for all of the fruit so we're going to buy 5 pieces of each fruit but for the watermelon 🍉, we only need two of it because it's too big and we won't be able to store all of them in our fridge. How do we do this?

```
const fridge = [
  { fruit: '🍉', amount: 1 },
  { fruit: '🍎', amount: 1 },
  { fruit: '🍐', amount: 1 },
  { fruit: '🍌', amount: 1 },
  { fruit: '🍌', amount: 1 }
];

const fridgeFullOfFruit = fridge.map(function (fruitObject) {
  if (fruitObject.fruit !== '🍉') {
    return {
      fruit: fruitObject.fruit,
      amount: 5
    };
  }
```

```
  return {
    fruit: fruitObject.fruit,
    amount: 2
  };
});
```

Let's digest what we've done above. We have created a new variable called fridgeFullOfFruit where we were going to store all of the fruit after doing groceries. Then we map (iterate) over the fruitObjects that are stored on the fridge variable and as we already know, the map method from the Array object it's a callback function and takes up to three arguments:

1. The element that's currently being iterated.
2. The index of the iteration.
3. The array that's being iterated.

In this particular scenario, we're only using the element that's currently being iterated so we can safely ignore the other two arguments, that's why our callback function has the following signature function(fruitObject) {}, because we're only using the current element in the iteration process.

Then we need to create the logic within the function that we want to apply to each of the elements in the array:

```
if (fruitObject.fruit !== '🍉') {
  return {
    fruit: fruitObject.fruit,
    amount: 5
  };
}

return {
  fruit: fruitObject.fruit,
  amount: 2
};
```

We're checking if the `fruit` property in the `fruitObject` **is** **not** a watermelon 🍉 and if it's not, we're going to return a `fruitObject` with the corresponding fruit and an amount of 5, which is the amount of fruit that we want to purchase for all of the fruits but watermelons 🍉 which should be an amount of 2.

For the sake of the example, we've made this code more explicit but we can make use of `arrow functions` with implicit return and a ternary operator to make this code even more compact.

```
const fridge = [
  { fruit: '🍎', amount: 1 },
  { fruit: '🍎', amount: 1 },
  { fruit: '🍐', amount: 1 },
```

```
  { fruit: '🍋', amount: 1 },
  { fruit: '🍌', amount: 1 }
];

const fridgeFullOfFruit = fridge.map((fruitObject) => ({
  ...fruitObject,
  amount: fruitObject.fruit !== '🍋' ? 5 : 2
}));
```

Filter an array to find elements

With the `filter(`**function**`(element, index))` method from the `Array` object we can iterate over the elements and return the ones that match the condition implemented on the callback function by returning `true` or `false`. This `filter` method will generate a new array with the results as the `map` method does.

Let's imagine we have the same `fruitObject` element that we had before in the `map` example.

```
const fruitObject = {
  fruit: '🍎',
  amount: 1
};
```

Let's fill the fridge with all of the corresponding fruit, but this time, some of them will have an amount of 0 (zero) and we're going to use this `amount` property to filter which elements we need to purchase so we can refill the fridge with.

```
const fridge = [
  { fruit: '🍎', amount: 0 },
  { fruit: '🍎', amount: 1 },
  { fruit: '💧', amount: 0 },
```

```
  { fruit: '🫐', amount: 1 },
  { fruit: '🍌', amount: 0 }
];
```

Now we need to `filter` all of these `fruitObjects` to determine which ones we need to purchase based on the `amount` property of each of this objects. How do we do this?

```
const fridge = [
  { fruit: '🍎', amount: 0 },
  { fruit: '🍅', amount: 1 },
  { fruit: '🍐', amount: 0 },
  { fruit: '🫐', amount: 1 },
  { fruit: '🍌', amount: 0 }
];

const shoppingList = fridge.filter(function (fruitObject) {
  if (fruitObject.amount === 0) {
    return true;
  }
  return false;
});
```

After filtering the `fridge` array with the given callback function, we will have a new array, `shoppingList` variable, containing the following:

```
[
  { fruit: '🍎', amount: 0 },
  { fruit: '🍐', amount: 0 },
  { fruit: '🍌', amount: 0 }
];
```

As a bonus, now we can map through this new shoppingList array to do some groceries!

```
const shoppingList = [
  { fruit: '🍎', amount: 0 },
  { fruit: '🍐', amount: 0 },
  { fruit: '🍌', amount: 0 }
];

const shoppingBasket = shoppingList.map((fruitObject) => ({
  ...fruitObject,
  amount: 5
}));
```

Now we have a shopping basket full of fresh and juicy fruit!

Reduce array values to a single value

With the reduce(**function**(accumulator, value, index), **initialValue**) method from the Array object we can iterate over the elements and return a single value. The second argument of the reduce function is initialValue, which will be used as the initial value for the accumulator. If you don't pass anything as this argument it will use the first value of the array and it will be skipped. My recommendation is to always pass something to this argument just to be more clear about what are you expecting to obtain at the end, plus if you use TypeScript you will get very nice IntelliSense about it.

Let's imagine once again that we have a fridge full of fruits shaped as a javascript object like the following:

```
const fruitObject = {
  fruit: '🍎',
  amount: 1
};
```

And now we would like to check how many fruits we have stored in the fridge in total. How do we do this?

```
const fridge = [
  { fruit: '🍎', amount: 2 },
  { fruit: '🍎', amount: 4 },
  { fruit: '🍐', amount: 1 },
  { fruit: '🍌', amount: 0 },
  { fruit: '🍇', amount: 3 }
];

const amountOfFruits = fridge.reduce(function (accumulated,
fruitObject) {
  return accumulated + fruitObject.amount;
}, 0);

amountOfFruits; // 2 + 4 + 1 + 0 + 3 = 10
```

The `reduce` method is a very handy function when you'd like to operate with arrays to obtain some value from them but you always have to remember that this function is very computational expensive so, if you can, you should try to avoid it if your CPU budget is low or you want to keep your application performing as best as possible. As a more performant alternative you can, for example, use a **for** loop like the following because it's worth it 🔥.

```
const fridge = [
  { fruit: '🍎', amount: 2 },
  { fruit: '🍎', amount: 4 },
  { fruit: '🍐', amount: 1 },
  { fruit: '🍌', amount: 0 },
```

```
  { fruit: '🍌', amount: 3 }
];

const amountOfFruits = 0;
const fruitsOnTheFridge = fridge.length;

for (let index = 0; index <= fruitsOnTheFridge; index++) {
  amountOfFruits += fridge[index].amount;
}

amountOfFruits; // 2 + 4 + 1 + 0 + 3 = 10
```

Creating an array from

With the **from**(arrayLikeObject, mapFunction) method from the Array object we can create a new Array from an iterable object.

```
const fruitsString = '🍎🍊🍐🍅🥑';
const fruits = Array.from(fruitsString);

fruits; // ['🍎', '🍊', '🍐', '🍅', '🥑']
```

In the example above we've used a string, in JavaScript, a string is an array-like object because it has a length property, but any object that has a length property or indexed elements can be used as well. Also, the Map and Set objects can be used here because they are iterable, therefore, perfectly valid.

The second argument of the **from** method is a callback function used to iterate over the elements after they're created, meaning that we can, for example, apply some logic to each of them, like the following:

```
const fruitsString = '🍎🍊🍐🍅🥑';
const fruits = Array.from(fruitsString, function (element) {
  return {
    fruit: element,
    amount: 5
```

```
  };
});

// {fruit: "🍎", amount: 5}
// {fruit: "🍑", amount: 5}
// {fruit: "🍐", amount: 5}
// {fruit: "🍈", amount: 5}
// {fruit: "🍌", amount: 5}
```

As we can see by the code snippet above, this method is very flexible and powerful and we've created an array of objects with some custom properties as we wanted.

Joining elements from an array into a string

With the `join(separator)` method from the `Array` object we can join the elements of an array into a string.

```
const fruits = ['🍎', '🍎', '🍐', '🥝', '🍌'];
const fruitsString = fruits.join();

fruitsString; // "🍎,🍎,🍐,🥝,🍌"
```

As we can tell by the code snippet above, the `join` method behaves a little weirdly when no `separator` argument is provided, this is because if we don't provide anything, it will use a `,` (coma) to separate the elements. If you would like to, for instance, have them all together, you could tell the `join` method to use an empty string "" as the separator.

```
const fruits = ['🍎', '🍎', '🍐', '🥝', '🍌'];
const fruitsString = fruits.join('');

fruitsString; // "🍎🍎🍐🥝🍌"
```

Checking if a value is an Array

With the `isArray(object)` method from the `Array` object, we can determine if the object passed as the main and only argument is an `Array`. This method will return `true` or `false` depending if the `object` meets the requirements or not.

Let's see how this actually behaves in different positive (`true`) scenarios:

```
Array.isArray([]); // true
Array.isArray(['🍎']); // true
Array.isArray(new Array()); // true
Array.isArray(new Array('🍎', '🍐', '🍎')); // true
Array.isArray(new Array(4)); // true
Array.isArray(Array.prototype); // true
```

Now let's see how this actually behaves in different negative (`false`) scenarios:

```
Array.isArray(); // false
Array.isArray({}); // false
Array.isArray(undefined); // false
Array.isArray(null); // false
Array.isArray(4); // false
Array.isArray('OTPfy'); // false
Array.isArray(true); // false
```

```
Array.isArray(false); // false
```

Flattening arrays

With the `flat(depth)` method from the `Array` object we can flatten an array that contains more arrays (sub-arrays) as values.

Let's imagine that our fridge contains different bags, and fruit is contained in each of those bags, and we would like to extract all the fruit from those bags too later on, do something with that fruit. How do we do this?

```
const fridge = [
  ['🍎', '🍎', '🍎', '🍎'], // apples bag
  ['🍐', '🍐'], // pears bag
  ['🍊'] // oranges bag
];

const allFruits = fridge.flat();

allFruits; // ["🍎", "🍎", "🍎", "🍎", "🍐", "🍐", "🍊"]
```

As we can see by the code snippet above, the `flat` method comes to be very handy when we want to obtain a single array without any nesting. Let's take a look at a more complex example:

```
const fridge = [
  ['🍎', '🍎', '🍎', '🍎'], // apples bag
  ['🍐', ['🍐', '🍐']], // pears bag
  [['🍊', ['🍊']], '🍊'] // oranges bag
];

const allFruits = fridge.flat();

allFruits; // ["🍎", "🍎", "🍎", "🍎", "🍐", ["🍐", "🍐"],
["🍊", ["🍊"]], "🍊"]
```

By looking at the output of the above code snippet we can determine that if we don't pass any numeric value to the `depth` argument of the `flat` method, it will only perform a flatten operation on the first-level row of array elements.

Let's now take a look at what happens if we pass a value to the `depth` property.

```
const fridge = [
  ['🍎', '🍎', '🍎', '🍎'], // apples bag
  ['🍐', ['🍐', '🍐']], // pears bag
  [['🍊', ['🍊']], '🍊'] // oranges bag
];

const allFruits = fridge.flat(2);

allFruits; // ["🍎", "🍎", "🍎", "🍎", "🍐", "🍐", "🍐",
"🍊", ["🍊"], "🍊"]
```

As we can see by the output, passing 2 as the `depth` property it flattens the array also on the second-level row of array elements but, our array is a three-level deep array. Let's flatten this by a `depth` of three and see what happens.

```
const fridge = [
  ['🍎', '🍎', '🍎', '🍎'], // apples bag
  ['🍐', ['🍐', '🍐']], // pears bag
  [['🍊', ['🍊']], '🍊'] // oranges bag
];

const allFruits = fridge.flat(3);

allFruits; // ["🍎", "🍎", "🍎", "🍎", "🍐", "🍐", "🍐",
"🍊", "🍊", "🍊"]
```

Great, we've achieved our objective of completely flattening the array into a single depth array!

Set

The `Set` object in JavaScript is a collection of unique values, represented as a data structure similar to an array. However, unlike arrays, sets do not allow duplicate values, and the values in a set have no specific order. Sets are useful for performing mathematical set operations, such as union, intersection, and difference.

Here's how to create and use a `Set` in JavaScript:

```javascript
// Creating a Set
const mySet = new Set();

// Adding values to the Set
mySet.add(1);
mySet.add(2);
mySet.add(3);
mySet.add(3); // This value will not be added to the set,
because it's a duplicate

// Checking the size of the Set
console.log(mySet.size); // Output: 3

// Checking if a value exists in the Set
console.log(mySet.has(2)); // Output: true
console.log(mySet.has(4)); // Output: false

// Removing values from the Set
mySet.delete(2);

// Clearing all values from the Set
mySet.clear();

// Initializing a Set with an array
const numbers = [1, 2, 3, 3, 4];
const uniqueNumbers = new Set(numbers);
console.log(uniqueNumbers.size); // Output: 4
```

The Set object provides several useful methods for working with sets, such as add for adding values, **delete** for removing values, clear for clearing all values, has for checking if a value exists in the set, and size for checking the number of values in the set.

One common use case of the Set object is to remove duplicates from an array. For instance:

```javascript
const numbers = [1, 2, 3, 3, 4];
const uniqueNumbers = new Set(numbers);
const backToArray = [...uniqueNumbers];
console.log(backToArray); // Output: [1, 2, 3, 4]
```

In this example, the Set constructor is used to remove duplicates from the numbers array, and the spread operator (...) is used to convert the set back into an array.

Map

The `Map` object in JavaScript is a collection of key-value pairs, represented as a data structure similar to an object or an associative array. Unlike objects, however, maps allow you to use any value (not just strings) as keys, and the keys in a map have no specific order. Maps are useful for maintaining a collection of related values, such as configuration options, or for counting the frequency of items in an array.

Here's how to create and use a `Map` in JavaScript:

```javascript
// Creating a Map
const myMap = new Map();

// Adding values to the Map
myMap.set("name", "John Doe");
myMap.set("age", 30);
myMap.set("city", "New York");

// Checking the size of the Map
console.log(myMap.size); // Output: 3

// Retrieving values from the Map
console.log(myMap.get("name")); // Output: "John Doe"
console.log(myMap.get("country")); // Output: undefined

// Removing values from the Map
myMap.delete("age");

// Clearing all values from the Map
myMap.clear();

// Initializing a Map with an array of key-value pairs
const options = [
  ["name", "John Doe"],
  ["age", 30],
  ["city", "New York"],
];
 config = new Map(options);
console.log(config.get("name")); // Output: "John Doe"
```

The `Map` object provides several useful methods for working with maps, such as `set` for adding values, `get` for retrieving values, **delete** for removing values, `clear` for clearing all values, and `size` for checking the number of key-value pairs in the map.

Intl.NumberFormat

`Intl.NumberFormat` is a built-in object in JavaScript that allows you to format and display numbers according to the conventions of a specific locale. It can be used to format numbers with different styles, such as decimal, currency, and percent, and it can be customized with options to control the number of digits, the use of grouping separators, and the use of a currency symbol.

Here's an example of using `Intl.NumberFormat` to format a number with the default (the one that's set as default on your system) locale:

```
const number = 123456.789;
const formatter = new Intl.NumberFormat();
console.log(formatter.format(number));  // 123,456.79
```

You can also specify a locale when creating the formatter:

```
const number = 123456.789;
const formatter = new Intl.NumberFormat('es-ES');
console.log(formatter.format(number));  // 123.456,789
```

In addition to locale, you can also specify options when creating the formatter, such as the style (decimal, currency, or percent) and currency:

```
const number = 123456.789;
const formatter = new Intl.NumberFormat('en-US', { style:
'currency', currency: 'USD' });
console.log(formatter.format(number));  // $123,456.79
```

You can also control the number of decimal places:

```
const number = 123456.789;
const formatter = new Intl.NumberFormat('en-US', {
minimumFractionDigits: 2, maximumFractionDigits: 5 });
console.log(formatter.format(number));  // 123,456.79000
```

Here's an example of using `Intl.NumberFormat` with the percent style:

```
const number = 0.5;
const formatter = new Intl.NumberFormat('en-US', { style:
'percent' });
console.log(formatter.format(number));  // 50%
```

In this example, we create a formatter with the locale en-US and specify the style as "percent". The number 0.5 is then passed to the formatter and it returns the string 50%.

`Intl.NumberFormat` is a useful tool for formatting numbers according to local conventions and standards, making your applications more user-friendly and culturally aware.

Intl.DateTimeFormat

`Intl.DateTimeFormat` is a built-in object in JavaScript that allows you to format and display dates and times according to the conventions of a specific locale.

Here's an example of using `Intl.DateTimeFormat` to format a date with the default (the one that's set as default on your system) locale:

```
const date = new Date();
const formatter = new Intl.DateTimeFormat();
```

```
console.log(formatter.format(date));   // 2/8/2023
```

You can also specify a locale when creating the formatter:

```
const date = new Date();
const formatter = new Intl.DateTimeFormat('es-ES');
console.log(formatter.format(date));   // 8/2/2023
```

In addition to locale, you can also specify options when creating the formatter, such as the format of the date and time:

```
const date = new Date();
const formatter = new Intl.DateTimeFormat('en-US', { year:
'numeric', month: 'short', day: 'numeric' });
console.log(formatter.format(date));   // Feb 8, 2023
```

Here is an example of formatting a date and time:

```
const date = new Date();
const formatter = new Intl.DateTimeFormat('en-US', { year:
'numeric', month: 'short', day: 'numeric', hour: 'numeric',
minute: 'numeric', second: 'numeric' });
```

```
console.log(formatter.format(date));  // Feb 8, 2023, 12:30:00
PM
```

`Intl.DateTimeFormat` is a useful tool for formatting dates and times according to local conventions and standards, making your applications more user-friendly and culturally aware.

Intl.RelativeTimeFormat

`Intl.RelativeTimeFormat` is a built-in object in JavaScript that allows you to format relative time in a human-readable string, according to the conventions of a specific locale.

Here's an example of using `Intl.RelativeTimeFormat` to format a relative time with the default locale:

```
const time = -5;
const unit = 'minute';
```

```
const formatter = new Intl.RelativeTimeFormat();
console.log(formatter.format(time, unit));  // -5 minutes ago
```

You can also specify a locale when creating the formatter:

```
const time = -5;
const unit = 'minute';
const formatter = new Intl.RelativeTimeFormat('es-ES');
console.log(formatter.format(time, unit));  // hace 5 minutos
```

In this example, we create a formatter with the locale es-ES and pass a time value and a unit to the formatter. The formatter returns a string with the relative time formatted according to the conventions of the French locale.

Here's an example of using `Intl.RelativeTimeFormat` with a custom style:

```
const time = -5;
const unit = 'minute';
const formatter = new Intl.RelativeTimeFormat('en-US', { style:
'narrow' });
console.log(formatter.format(time, unit));  // -5m
```

In this example, we create a formatter with the locale en-US and specify the style as narrow. The time value and unit are then passed to the formatter, and it returns a string with the relative time in an abbreviated format.

`Intl.RelativeTimeFormat` is a useful tool for formatting relative times in a way that is culturally appropriate and makes your applications more user-friendly and culturally aware.

Intl.ListFormat

`Intl.ListFormat` is a built-in object in JavaScript that allows you to format lists of items into a human-readable string, according to the conventions of a specific locale.

Here's an example of using `Intl.ListFormat` to format a list of items with the default locale:

```
const items = ['apple', 'banana', 'cherry'];
const formatter = new Intl.ListFormat();
```

```
console.log(formatter.format(items));  // apple, banana, and
cherry
```

You can also specify a locale when creating the formatter:

```
const items = ['manzana', 'platano', 'cereza'];
const formatter = new Intl.ListFormat('es-ES');
console.log(formatter.format(items));  // manzana, platano y
cereza
```

In this example, we create a formatter with the locale es-ES and pass an array of items to the formatter. The formatter returns a string with the items formatted according to the conventions of the Spanish locale.

`Intl.ListFormat` is a useful tool for formatting lists of items in a way that is culturally appropriate, making your applications more user-friendly and culturally aware.

Promises

A `Promise` in JavaScript is an object representing the eventual completion or failure of an asynchronous operation. It provides a way to register callbacks to be notified when the operation has been completed or failed.

Here's an example of using a Promise to handle the result of an asynchronous operation:

```
const fetchData = () => {
  return new Promise((resolve, reject) => {
```

```
    setTimeout(() => {
      resolve('Data fetched successfully');
    }, 2000);
  });
};

fetchData().then(data => {
  console.log(data); // Data fetched successfully
});
```

In this example, we create a `Promise` object by passing a function to its constructor. The function takes two arguments, `resolve` and `reject`, which are used to signal the completion or failure of the operation. After two seconds, we use `resolve` to signal that the operation has been completed successfully and pass the result `'Data fetched successfully'` to the `then` method.

Here's an example of using a Promise to handle an error:

```
const fetchData = () => {
  return new Promise((resolve, reject) => {
    setTimeout(() => {
      reject(new Error('Data fetch failed'));
    }, 2000);
  });
};
```

```
fetchData().catch(error => {
  console.error(error); // Error: Data fetch failed
});
```

In this example, we create a `Promise` object in the same way as before, but this time, after two seconds, we use `reject` to signal that the operation has failed and pass an error to the **catch** method.

Promises are commonly used in JavaScript development to handle asynchronous operations, such as fetching data from an API, reading or writing to a file, or performing complex calculations. They allow you to write asynchronous code that is easier to read and maintain, making your applications more robust and scalable.

Async/Await

`async/await` is a more modern way of handling asynchronous operations in JavaScript and is built on top of Promises. It provides a way to write asynchronous code that is more concise and easier to read.

Here's an example of using `async/await` to handle the result of an asynchronous operation:

```
const fetchData = () => {
  return new Promise((resolve, reject) => {
```

```
    setTimeout(() => {
      resolve('Data fetched successfully');
    }, 2000);
  });
};

const handleData = async () => {
  const data = await fetchData();
  console.log(data); // Data fetched successfully
};

handleData();
```

In this example, we create a function `handleData` that is declared as **async**. This means that the function returns a Promise and can use **await** to wait for the completion of an asynchronous operation. We call the `fetchData` function, which returns a Promise, and use **await** to wait for the Promise to resolve. Once the Promise has resolved, the value is stored in the `data` variable, which we can then use in the rest of the function.

Here's an example of using async/await to handle an error:

```
const fetchData = () => {
  return new Promise((resolve, reject) => {
    setTimeout(() => {
      reject(new Error('Data fetch failed'));
    }, 2000);
  });
```

```
};

const handleData = async () => {
  try {
    const data = await fetchData();
    console.log(data);
  } catch (error) {
    console.error(error); // Error: Data fetch failed
  }
};

handleData();
```

In this example, we create the `handleData` function in the same way as before, but this time we use a `try...catch` block to handle any errors that occur when waiting for the Promise to resolve. If an error occurs, the `catch` block is executed, and we can use `console.error` to log the error.

`async/await` is another way of handling asynchronous operations in JavaScript, and is a great way to write asynchronous code that is concise and easier to read. It provides a way to write asynchronous code that is more like synchronous code, making it easier to understand and maintain.

The Prototype

In JavaScript, the prototype is an object that is associated with every function and object and is used to provide a mechanism for inheritance and shared properties. When an object is created, it inherits all of the properties and methods of its prototype.

Every function in JavaScript has a prototype property, which is initially set to an empty object. You can add properties and methods to this object to create a shared set of functionality that can be inherited by objects created from that function.

Here's an example of how you can use the prototype to create an object with shared properties and methods:

```javascript
function Person(name, age) {
  this.name = name;
  this.age = age;
}

Person.prototype.sayHello = function() {
  console.log(`Hello, my name is ${this.name}`);
};

const john = new Person('John Doe', 30);
const jane = new Person('Jane Doe', 28);

john.sayHello(); // Output: Hello, my name is John Doe
jane.sayHello(); // Output: Hello, my name is Jane Doe
```

In this example, we create a `Person` function and add a `sayHello` method to its prototype. We then create two objects, `john` and `jane`, using the `Person` function as a constructor. Both `john` and `jane` inherit the `sayHello` method from the `Person` prototype and can use it to print a message.

It's important to note that the prototype is a shared object, so any changes to the prototype will be reflected in all objects that inherit from it. This can be both a powerful and a dangerous feature, so it's important to use it carefully and with a good understanding of how it works.

The `this` keyword

The `this` keyword in JavaScript refers to the object that is currently executing the code that contains the `this` reference. The value of `this` depends on how a function is called, and it can be used to access and modify the properties of the object that is executing the code. Here are some examples of how this can be used in JavaScript

Example 1: In a method, `this` refers to the object that contains the method.

```
const person = {
  name: 'John Doe',
  age: 30,
  sayHello: function() {
    console.log(`Hello, my name is ${this.name}`);
  }
};

person.sayHello(); // Output: Hello, my name is John Doe
```

Example 2: In an event handler, `this` refers to the element that triggered the event.

```
const button = document.getElementById('myButton');
button.addEventListener('click', function() {
  console.log(`Button with id "${this.id}" was clicked`);
});
```

Example 3: In a constructor, `this` refers to the object being created

```
function Person(name, age) {
  this.name = name;
  this.age = age;
}

const john = new Person('John Doe', 30);
```

```
console.log(john.name); // Output: John Doe
```

One of the main uses of `this` is to access and modify the properties of the object that is executing the code. For example, in the first example, the `sayHello` method uses this to access the name property of the person object.

One of the biggest challenges with `this` is understanding its value, as it can change depending on how a function is called. This can lead to unexpected results and can be a source of confusion, especially for developers who are new to JavaScript.

In addition, `this` can be changed using methods like `bind`, `call`, and `apply`, which can be useful in certain cases but can also lead to further confusion if not used carefully.

Overall, the `this` keyword is a powerful feature of JavaScript, but it can be challenging to understand and use correctly. It's important to have a good understanding of how this works, and to use it carefully and with consideration for its potential pitfalls.

The `bind` method

The `bind` method in JavaScript is used to create a new function that has its `this` value set to a specific object. This can be useful when you want to pass a method as a callback, but need to ensure that this refers to a specific object inside the callback.

Here's an example of how you can use `bind` to set the value of this inside a method:

```
const person = {
```

```
  name: 'John Doe',
  sayHello: function() {
    console.log(`Hello, my name is ${this.name}`);
  }
};

const sayHello = person.sayHello;
sayHello(); // Output: Hello, my name is undefined

const boundSayHello = sayHello.bind(person);
boundSayHello(); // Output: Hello, my name is John Doe
```

In the example above, we first create an object person with a name property and a sayHello method that logs a greeting. We then assign the sayHello method to a variable sayHello, and call that variable as a standalone function. Because the sayHello method is now being called as a standalone function, **this** no longer refers to the person object, and instead refers to the global object (or undefined in strict mode), so the output is undefined.

To fix this, we use the bind method to create a new function boundSayHello that has its **this** value set to the person object. When we call boundSayHello, this refers to person, so the output is as expected.

bind is just one of several ways to change the value of this in JavaScript, but it can be a convenient and flexible way to ensure that a specific object is referenced by **this** inside a function.

The `call` method

The `call` method in JavaScript allows you to invoke a function with a specific **this** value and arguments. Unlike the `bind` method, which returns a new function with a pre-bound **this** value, the `call` method immediately invokes the function with the specified **this** value and arguments.

Here's an example of how you can use the `call` method:

```
const person = {
  name: 'John Doe',
  sayHello: function(greeting) {
    console.log(`${greeting}, my name is ${this.name}`);
  }
};

person.sayHello.call({ name: 'Jane Doe' }, 'Hi');
// Output: Hi, my name is Jane Doe
```

In the example above, we have an object person with a name property and a sayHello method that logs a greeting. We use the call method to invoke the sayHello method, passing an object { name: 'Jane Doe' } as the this value, and the string 'Hi' as the first argument. The call method immediately invokes the sayHello method with the specified this value and arguments, so the output is 'Hi, my name is Jane Doe'.

The call method can be useful when you need to reuse a function with different this values and arguments, or when you want to invoke a method as a standalone function with a specific this value.

The call method is one of several ways to change the value of this in JavaScript, and can be a powerful tool for managing function invocation and method reuse.

The apply method

The `apply` method in JavaScript allows you to invoke a function with a specific **this** value and an array of arguments. Like the `call` method, the `apply` method immediately invokes the function with the specified **this** value and arguments. The difference is that the `apply` method takes an array of arguments, while the `call` method takes a comma-separated list of arguments.

Here's an example of how you can use the `apply` method:

```javascript
const person = {
  name: 'John Doe',
  sayHello: function(greeting) {
    console.log(`${greeting}, my name is ${this.name}`);
  }
};

person.sayHello.apply({ name: 'Jane Doe' }, ['Hi']);
// Output: Hi, my name is Jane Doe
```

In the example above, we have an object person with a name property and a sayHello method that logs a greeting. We use the apply method to invoke the sayHello method, passing an object { name: 'Jane Doe' } as the this value, and an array ['Hi'] as the second argument. The apply method immediately invokes the sayHello method with the specified this value and arguments, so the output is 'Hi, my name is Jane Doe'.

The apply method can be useful when you need to reuse a function with different this values and arguments, or when you want to invoke a method as a standalone function with a specific this value and an array of arguments.

The apply method is one of several ways to change the value of this in JavaScript, and can be a powerful tool for managing function invocation and method reuse.

Template literals

Template literals are a feature of ECMAScript 6 (ES6) that allow you to easily embed expressions within string literals. They are indicated by using backticks (`` ` ``) instead of single or double quotes.

Here's an example of how you can use template literals:

```
const name = 'John Doe';
const message = `Hello, my name is ${name}`;
console.log(message);
```

```
// Output: Hello, my name is John Doe
```

In the example above, we use a template literal to embed the value of the name variable within a string. The expressions within the template literal (indicated by ${}) are evaluated and the results are concatenated with the surrounding string. The result is a string with the evaluated expression values.

Template literals also support multiline strings, making it easy to write strings that span multiple lines:

```
const poem = `Roses are red,
Violets are blue,
Sugar is sweet,
And so are you.`;
```

Template literals provide a convenient and readable way to embed expressions within strings, making them a useful tool for string manipulation and template rendering.

Iterating objects with the for...in loop

The `for...in` loop in JavaScript is used to iterate over the enumerable properties of an object. It's important to note that `for...in` loops are designed for objects, not for arrays. For arrays, it's recommended to use the `for...of` loop or the traditional `for` loop.

Here's an example of using the `for...in` loop to iterate over the properties of an object:

```
const person = {
```

```
    name: 'John Doe',
    age: 30,
    occupation: 'Developer'
};

for (const property in person) {
    console.log(`${property}: ${person[property]}`);
}
```

In this example, we have an object called person with three properties: name, age, and occupation. We use the for...in loop to iterate over the properties of the person object. The property variable is set to each property in turn, and we use the square bracket notation to access the value of the property. The output of this code would be:

```
name: John Doe
age: 30
occupation: Developer
```

It's important to note that for...in loops will include properties that are inherited from the object's prototype, so it's recommended to use a hasOwnProperty check to ensure that only the object's own properties are processed:

```javascript
for (const property in person) {
  if (person.hasOwnProperty(property)) {
    console.log(`${property}: ${person[property]}`);
  }
}
```

The `for...in` loop can be useful for iterating over the properties of an object, but it's important to use it correctly and with caution, as it will include properties that are inherited from the object's prototype.

Closures

Closures are a fundamental concept in JavaScript and refer to a function that has access to variables in its outer scope even after the outer function has returned. Closures are created when a function is defined inside another function and have access to the variables and functions defined in the outer scope.

Here's an example of a closure in JavaScript:

```
function outerFunction() {
```

```
let outerVariable = 'I am the outer variable';

function innerFunction() {
  console.log(outerVariable);
}

return innerFunction;
}

const closure = outerFunction();
closure();
// Output: I am the outer variable
```

In the example above, the innerFunction has access to the outerVariable even after the outerFunction has returned. When we call outerFunction, it returns the innerFunction and assigns it to the variable closure. When we call closure, it has access to outerVariable and logs its value to the console.

Closures are used to keep variables alive and accessible even after the function that created them has returned. They are commonly used to create private variables and methods that are not accessible from the outside, to preserve states across multiple invocations, and to implement functional programming patterns. Closures are also important for implementing higher-order functions, which are functions that take other functions as arguments or return functions as values.

Here are some more details about closures in JavaScript:

1. Closures have access to the outer scope even after the outer function has returned. They keep a reference to the variables in the outer scope, and any changes to those variables will persist across multiple invocations of the closure.

2. Closures can only access variables that are defined in their outer scope. They cannot access variables defined inside the closure itself.

3. Closures can be used to create private variables and methods. By returning an anonymous function from within another function, you can create a closure that has access to the variables and functions defined in the outer scope. The closure can use these variables and functions as private variables and methods.

4. Closures can preserve the state across multiple invocations. By storing values in the variables defined in the outer scope, you can maintain the state between invocations of the closure.

5. Closures can be used to implement functional programming patterns. For example, you can use closures to implement the curry and compose functions, which allow you to create new functions by composing existing functions.

Here's an example of a closure that implements a private variable and method:

```
function createCounter() {
  let count = 0;

  return {
    increment: function() {
      count++;
    },
    getCount: function() {
      return count;
    }
  };
}

const counter = createCounter();
counter.increment();
console.log(counter.getCount());
// Output: 1
```

In the example above, `createCounter` returns an object with two methods: `increment` and `getCount`. The `increment` method increments the value of `count`, and the `getCount` method returns the value of `count`. The `count` variable is defined in the outer scope and is only accessible from within the closure. This makes it a private variable that cannot be accessed from outside the closure.

Printed in Great Britain
by Amazon

21521854R00106